# Sea Turtles

TEXT BY MARY JO RHODES AND DAVID HALL
PHOTOGRAPHS BY DAVID HALL

Undersea Encounters

**Children's Press®**
A Division of Scholastic Inc.
New York   Toronto   London   Auckland   Sydney
Mexico City   New Delhi   Hong Kong
Danbury, Connecticut

Library of Congress Cataloging-in-Publication Data

Rhodes, Mary Jo, 1957-
    Sea turtles / Mary Jo Rhodes and David Hall; photographs by David Hall.— 1st ed.
        p. cm. — (Undersea encounters)
    Includes bibliographical references and index.
    ISBN 0-516-24391-8 (lib. bdg.)          0-516-25353-0 (pbk.)
    1. Sea turtles—Juvenile literature.  I. Hall, David, 1943 Oct. 2- II. Title. III. Series.
    QL666.C536R55 2005
    597.92'8—dc22
                                    2005000354

*To the scientists, conservationists, government workers, and ordinary people everywhere*
*who are working hard to save sea turtles from extinction.*
*—D.H.*
*To my sister, Renée, and to my niece, Alia*
*—M.J.R.*

All photographs © 2005 David Hall except: Corbis Images: 43 (Bob Krist), 40 (Jeffery L. Rotman); Seapics.com: 14, 15 (Franco Banfi), 4, 5, 33 (Mark Conlin), 41 (Mark Conlin/ USFWS/FWC), 13 (Susan Dabritz-Yuen), 9, 23 bottom inset, 24 inset, 24, 25, 28, 34, 35 inset, 37 (Doug Perrine), 42 (Mark Strickland), 6, 31, 32 (James D. Watt).

Sea turtles have been on Earth since before the dinosaurs!
pg. **17**

Sea turtles "fly" underwater.
pg. **20**

# Sea Turtles

Sea turtles are one of just a few reptiles that swim in the ocean.
pg. **14**

A hatchling loggerhead sea turtle makes its way out of the shell.

# chapter 1

# A Sea Turtle's Life Begins

Curled up tightly inside an egg, a baby sea turtle is ready to break free. She pokes at the leathery shell with her egg tooth, a pointy knob on the end of her beak. An opening appears in the shell. Soon a small head pushes out. It is followed by a dark body with four flippers and a short tail.

Nearby, other **hatchlings** (HACH-lings) have already broken free of their shells. They must all dig through several

5

A baby green sea turtle is
about to enter the water for
the first time.

6

feet of sand to reach the surface. It takes up to three days of hard work. At last, the baby turtles stick their heads up through the sand.

## A Race to the Sea

The baby turtle scrambles toward the water. Enemies are everywhere. She must reach the water quickly to survive. At last the baby turtle reaches wet sand near the breaking waves.

She plunges into the waves, and paddles toward the open sea. The tiny hatchling swims for several days. She does not stop to eat or rest. Finally, she finds food and shelter in a raft of floating seaweed.

## Turtle Fact

Many baby sea turtles die before they reach the water. They are eaten by seabirds, crabs, and other animals. Perhaps only one in a thousand will survive to reach adulthood.

A hatchling hawksbill sea turtle rests on the surface.

A hatchling loggerhead turtle
takes shelter in floating seaweed.

The young turtle will live at sea for the next
few years. If she survives to become an adult, she
will one day return to the same beach where she
was hatched. There, she will lay her own eggs.

The head and flippers of
a sea turtle are protected
by tough scales.

# chapter 2

# Ocean-going Reptiles

Sea turtles are **reptiles** (REP-tiles) just like snakes, crocodiles, and lizards. Like most reptiles they breathe air, have scaly skin, and lay eggs.

But sea turtles are different from other reptiles in some ways. For example, sea turtles don't have teeth. Instead, they have sharp beaks and strong jaws for cracking open lobsters and other **prey** (PRAY).

A sleeping sea turtle can hold its breath for more than one hour.

## Holding Their Breath

Like all reptiles, sea turtles have lungs for breathing in air. They don't have gills and can't breathe underwater like a fish.

Most of the time, a sea turtle needs to come to the surface once every ten or fifteen minutes to breathe. But when it is sleeping, a sea turtle can hold its breath for more than an hour.

## Staying Warm

Almost all reptiles are cold-blooded. This means that their body temperature varies with their surroundings. Most sea turtles live in **tropical** (TROP-uh-kuhl) seas. The warm water helps them to keep an ideal body temperature.

Sea turtles can't move around much when their bodies are cold. They sometimes need the sun to warm themselves. This behavior is called basking. Most sea turtles bask while floating on the surface of the water. Only one **species** (SPEE-seez), the green sea turtle, sometimes leaves the ocean and basks on a beach.

Green sea turtles sometimes come ashore to warm themselves in the sun.

# Other Ocean Reptiles

During the time of the dinosaurs, many kinds of reptiles lived in the ocean. But almost all of these reptiles became extinct at the same time as the dinosaurs did, around 65 million years ago. Besides sea turtles, only a few other kinds of reptiles now swim in the ocean.

## Saltwater crocodiles

Saltwater crocodiles spend all of their lives in or near the ocean. They usually come ashore only to sun themselves and to lay eggs. Saltwater crocodiles are fierce **predators** (PRED-uh-turs). They can reach a length of more than 20 feet (6 meters).

## Sea snakes

Sea snakes are more at home in the ocean than any other reptile. Some sea snakes come ashore to sun themselves or to lay eggs, but most spend their whole lives in the ocean. They even give birth to their young without ever leaving the water!

## Marine iguanas

Marine iguanas are the only lizards that swim in the ocean. They enter the sea to feed on seaweed growing on the ocean floor. Marine iguanas live in the Galápagos Islands, off the Pacific coast of South America.

Sea turtles are some of the most ancient reptiles on Earth.

# chapter 3

# Shells and Flippers

Sea turtles have been on earth for millions of years. The ancient ancestors of sea turtles were giant land turtles. Around the time of the dinosaurs, about 175 million years ago, some of these land turtles **adapted** (uh-DAPT-ed) to life in the ocean.

Scientists don't know why some turtles left the land for the sea. Land turtles usually have thick, heavy shells. These shells protect them from predators and from the hot sun. But it is difficult to swim and dive with a large, heavy shell. So sea turtles' shells changed over time, as they adapted to life in the sea. Their shells became lighter and more streamlined.

## A Turtle's Shell

The upper part of a turtle's shell is attached to its spine and ribs. This upper shell is called the **carapace** (KARE-uh-pase). The bottom part of the shell is called the **plastron** (PLAS-tron). It protects the turtle's belly. The carapace and plastron are connected to form a complete shell.

The turtle's head and legs are covered with scales. The hard shell is covered with larger horny plates called **scutes** (SKOOTS). These scutes form a pattern on the turtle's back. Each species of sea turtle has a different pattern.

plastron

# Carapace, Plastron, and Scutes

A turtle's shell has two main parts, the carapace and the plastron. Both parts are connected to form a complete shell. The turtle's head, legs, and tail poke out of openings in the shell. While a land turtle can pull its limbs and head completely inside its shell, sea turtles cannot do this.

carapace

scutes

## Flying Underwater

Sea turtles' land ancestors had clawed feet. Over time, their feet developed into large, paddlelike flippers. A sea turtle can swim slowly by using its front flippers like oars. It can also swim quickly by flapping them like wings. When swimming fast, a sea turtle looks like it is flying underwater.

Sea turtles use their large front flippers to "fly" through the water.

# Look Out!

Adult sea turtles don't have many natural enemies because of their large size and protective shell. They are powerful swimmers and can escape from most predators. But sometimes a shark can sneak up on a turtle from behind and take a big bite. A large shark might even kill and eat a sea turtle.

This turtle lost a rear flipper and part of its shell as a result of a shark bite.

# Different Kinds of Sea Turtles

There are seven species of sea turtles. They have a lot in common with one another, but they also have some important differences.

# Loggerhead Turtle

Loggerheads are named for their large heads. They have thick, powerful jaws that are used to crack open the shells of snails, lobsters, and other prey.

Loggerhead turtles travel farther than most ocean animals. Some loggerheads swim across the Pacific Ocean from Japan to Mexico—more than 5,600 miles (9,000 kilometers)!

# Green Turtle

The green turtle is the second-largest sea turtle. It does not look green, but is named for the color of its fat. Green turtles eat mostly plants such as seagrass and seaweed. They have been widely hunted because of their tasty meat.

# Leatherback Turtle

The leatherback is the largest species of sea turtle. Its shell can reach a length of 8.4 feet (2.6 m). It may weigh up to 2,000 pounds (900 kilograms). That's as long as a sofa and heavier than a horse!

The leatherback is the only sea turtle without a hard shell. Instead, it has an

# Australian Flatback Turtle

The Australian flatback is a medium-size sea turtle. It has an unusual carapace that is turned up along the edges. Flatbacks live near Australia. They do not migrate long distances.

## Hawksbill Turtle

The hawksbill turtle is named for its beak. Like the bill of a hawk, its beak is pointed and curved.

For centuries, hawksbill turtles were hunted for their beautiful shells. Because hawksbills have become endangered, it is now illegal to hunt them.

## Olive Ridley and Kemp's Ridley Turtles

Ridleys (above) are the smallest of the sea turtle species. They usually weigh about as much as a large dog. The Kemp's Ridley is the rarest and most **endangered** (en-DAYN-jurd) of all sea turtles.

Both Ridley species have an unusual nesting behavior. It is called arribada. *Arribada* is a Spanish word meaning "arrival." During an arribada, hundreds or even thousands of nesting females come ashore at the same time to lay their eggs.

25

Hawksbill turtles often make their homes on coral reefs.

# chapter 4

# Turtles On the Move

Some adult sea turtles live in one place for most of their lives. Other turtles **migrate** (MYE-grate) to warmer water in the winter. Still other species, such as leatherbacks, wander the open ocean. During the mating season, many sea turtles migrate long distances to reach nesting areas.

## Traveling Alone

Sea turtles usually travel alone. They spend part of each day swimming around and

A loggerhead turtle uses its powerful jaws to break open the shell of a large sea snail.

looking for food. A hawksbill turtle eats **sponges** (SPUNJZ) that grow on **coral reefs** (KOR-uhl REEFS). A green turtle grazes in undersea meadows, eating the seagrass. Loggerhead turtles search for crunchy shellfish such as crabs and lobsters. At night sea turtles often find a favorite rocky ledge or cave to sleep in.

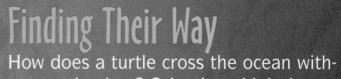

# Finding Their Way

How does a turtle cross the ocean without getting lost? Scientists think that sea turtles have a "magnetic" sense, like a compass. This helps them figure out their location and direction. They probably also use other clues. The smell of the air, the taste of the water, and the position of the sun may help them find their way.

## Riding with Sea Turtles

Sea turtles often pick up passengers as they roam. These passengers get a free ride as the turtle swims from place to place. Shelled animals called barnacles, and plants called algae may grow on a turtle's shell. Sometimes harmful animals called **parasites** (PA-ruh-sites) attach themselves to the turtle's skin.

Barnacles are growing on the shell of this hawksbill turtle.

Sea turtles living on a coral reef sometimes visit a cleaning station. There, "cleaner fish" remove and eat algae and small creatures on the turtle's shell and skin. The turtle can swim faster and will be healthier with a clean shell.

In return for helping the turtle, the cleaner fish gets a tasty meal. Both the turtle and the cleaner fish are better off as a result.

A "cleaner fish" eats the algae growing on the skin of a green turtle.

## Turtle Fact

Some land turtles have lived more than 150 years. Sea turtles can live a long time too, possibly 60 to 80 years or more.

A female sea turtle mates
with a male before coming
ashore to lay her eggs.
Mating takes place
underwater.

# chapter 5

# Nesting Turtles

For up to twenty years, a young female sea turtle never leaves the water. During this time, she is growing. Soon she will be ready to **mate**. When the time is right, she returns to the same beach where she was hatched many years before.

There she mates with a male turtle in the water, just off the shore. Later, she pulls herself out of the ocean. This is difficult and dangerous. Her flippers are made for swimming, not for

Female sea turtles must come ashore to lay their eggs.

walking. She will not be able to outrun a hungry predator.

**A Nest in the Sand**

The female turtle crawls out of the water to dig a nest. It is there that she will lay her eggs. She must crawl far out onto the shore so that the nest will stay dry. She uses her front flippers to create a deep pit around herself.

Then the sea turtle scoops out a smaller hole in the bottom of the pit. To do this, she uses her hind flippers. This smaller hole is called an egg chamber. She lays about one hundred eggs in this smaller hole.

**Turtle Fact**

Nesting turtles usually come ashore at sunset or after dark. It is cooler then, and predators can't see them as easily.

After first digging with her front flippers, a female sea turtle uses her hind flippers to dig out the egg chamber.

Female green turtles lay an average of about 100 eggs.

35

## Protecting the Nest

When the sea turtle is finished laying her eggs, she covers them carefully. She fills in the egg chamber and the larger pit with sand. She hides the location of the nest by smoothing over the sand. Animals, such as raccoons and dogs, might want to dig up the eggs and eat them.

## A New Life Begins

With her task completed, the sea turtle crawls slowly back to the water. The eggs will hatch in six to twelve weeks. The baby sea turtles will break out of their eggs and dig up through the sand. One night, under the cover of darkness, they will scramble quickly toward the water.

Young sea turtles live in the open ocean for five to ten years after hatching. Many of them later return to shallow water.

Hatchling green turtles emerge from their underground nest and head for the ocean.

## Turtle Fact

Will it be a boy or a girl? It depends on the temperature of the sand. If the nest is cool, the babies will be males. Warmer sand results in female hatchlings.

Hawksbill turtles, like the one in this photograph, are now critically endangered.

# chapter 6

# Sea Turtles in Danger

Once there were tens of millions of sea turtles swimming in the ocean. But over the centuries, people captured large numbers of them. The turtles were hunted for their shells, eggs, and meat. Today there are far fewer left of all species, especially hawksbills, leatherbacks, and Kemp's Ridleys.

These sea turtle species are considered to be endangered. Most countries, including the United States, now have laws protecting sea turtles.

A hawksbill turtle is caught in a net.

## Danger at Sea

Many sea turtles become trapped in fishing nets and drown. Thousands of turtles are caught and killed each year by longlines. These are fishing lines several miles long with many hooks.

Garbage floating at sea is dangerous to sea turtles. A sea turtle may become tangled up and drown in fishing line that's been thrown away in the ocean. Sea turtles sometimes eat plastic bags, mistaking them for jellyfish. A turtle that swallows a plastic bag or other garbage may become sick and die.

### Turtle Fact

To help protect sea turtles, shrimp fishermen use special nets. These nets have a trapdoor in the back. A turtle that accidentally swims into this net can make an easy escape.

# Learning About Sea Turtles

Scientists need to learn more about sea turtles in order to protect them. They can do this by using **satellite transmitters** (SAT-uh-lite trans-MITRS). Scientists attach the transmitter to a turtle's shell. As the turtle swims, the scientists receive signals from the device that track the turtle's movements. In this way, scientists learn more about the turtle's behavior.

## Danger on Land

Sea turtles also face danger on land. Sometimes people build sea walls to protect nearby homes from storms. However, the walls may prevent turtles from nesting.

Also, bright lights near the beach can confuse hatchlings. They may crawl away from the water rather than toward it. In some parts of the world, people still dig up sea turtle eggs to eat or to sell.

Sea turtle eggs are for sale in a street market in Indonesia.

An injured sea turtle receives treatment at a "turtle hospital."

## Helping Sea Turtles

Today, people are working hard to save sea turtles. It is illegal to sell sea turtle products in most countries. Some nesting beaches are guarded to protect female turtles and their eggs. Aquariums and "turtle hospitals" help heal sick and wounded turtles.

Sea turtles have been on earth for millions of years. If we all work together to protect them, sea turtles will be around for many years to come.

# Glossary

**adapt** (uh-DAPT) when an animal or plant species changes over many generations to make it better able to survive and reproduce. *(pg. 17)*

**carapace** (KARE-uh-pase) the top half of a turtle's shell. *(pg. 18)*

**coral reef** (KOR-uhl REEF) a tropical, shallow, ocean environment created by many generations of tiny animals called corals. *(pg. 28)*

**endangered** (en-DAYN-jurd) an animal species is endangered when there are very few of them left alive. *(pg. 25)*

**hatchling** (HACH-ling) a turtle that recently came out of an egg. *(pg. 5)*

**mate** when animals come together to produce offspring. *(pg. 33)*

**migrate** (MYE-grate) to move from one region to another, usually for the purpose of feeding or breeding, or because of seasonal weather changes. *(pg. 27)*

**parasite** (PA-ruh-site) a creature that lives on or in another living thing, and causes it harm. *(pg. 30)*

**plastron** (PLAS-tron) the bottom half of a turtle's shell. *(pg. 18)*

**predator** (PRED-uh-tur) an animal that hunts and kills other animals for food. *(pg. 14)*

**prey** (PRAY) an animal that is hunted and killed for food. *(pg. 11)*

**reptile** (REP-tile) animal with a backbone that has scales, breathes air, and usually lays eggs. *(pg. 11)*

**satellite transmitter** (SAT-uh-lite trans-MITR) a small box that researchers place on a sea turtle's carapace that sends signals to a satellite in space. The signals can tell researchers where the turtle is located. *(pg. 41)*

**scutes** (SKOOTS) the individual sections or plates that cover a sea turtle's shell. *(pg. 18)*

**species** (SPEE-seez) a particular kind of animal or plant. *(pg. 13)*

**sponge** (SPUHNJ) a simple sea animal that has no internal organs. *(pg. 28)*

**tropical** (TROP-uh-kuhl) located in the warmest parts of the world, near the equator. *(pg. 12)*

# Learn More About Sea Turtles

## Books

Bair, Diane, and Pamela Wright. *Sea Turtle Watching: A How-To Guide.* Mankato, MN: Capstone Books, 2000.

Lasky, Kathryn. *Interrupted Journey: Saving Endangered Sea Turtles.* New York: Candlewick Press, 2001.

Perrine, Doug. *Sea Turtles of the World.* Stillwater, Minn.: Voyageur Press, 2003.

## Organizations and Online Sites

National Save The Sea Turtle Foundation
(www.savetheseaturtle.org)

Caribbean Conservation Corporation
(www.cccturtle.org)

Sea Turtle Restoration Project
(www.seaturtles.org)

Turtle Trax
(www.turtles.org)

# Index

# About the Authors

After earning degrees in zoology and medicine, **David Hall** has worked for the past twenty-five years as both a wildlife photojournalist and a physician. David's articles and photographs have appeared in hundreds of calendars, books, and magazines, including *National Geographic, Smithsonian, Natural History,* and *Ranger Rick.* His underwater images have won many major awards including *Nature's Best,* BBC Wildlife Photographer of the Year and Festival Mondial de l'Image Sous-Marine.

**Mary Jo Rhodes** has been interested in sea turtles ever since she and her family saw a loggerhead turtle lay her eggs on a beach at Canaveral National Seashore in Florida.

She received her M.S. in Library Service from Columbia University and was a librarian for the Brooklyn Public Library. She later worked for ten years in children's book publishing in New York City. Mary Jo lives with her husband, John Rounds, and two teenage sons, Jeremy and Tim, in Hoboken, New Jersey.

# About the Consultant

**Doug Perrine** has a master's degree in marine biology and has participated in scientific research on whales, sharks, and sea turtles. He has worked as a consultant for films produced by the National Geographic Society and the Discovery Channel. Doug is the author of seven books and numerous articles on marine life, including *Sea Turtles of the World,* published by Voyageur Press.